AF674286

Junkets

poems

Joseph Hart

ISBN: 978-81-8253-859-7

First Edition: 2022
Rs. 200/-

Cyberwit.net
HIG 45 Kaushambi Kunj, Kalindipuram
Allahabad - 211011 (U.P.) India
http://www.cyberwit.net
Tel: +(91) 9415091004
E-mail: info@cyberwit.net

Printed at Repro India Limited.

Maxx

CONTENTS

Junkets

Junkets gave the world
Imaginary sweets.
It's all imagination,
Johnny Keats!

Cats & Poets

When a cat's in trouble,
It's his lot
To cry until he's rescued,
Or he's not.

When a poet's stymied,
What to do? -
If it isn't pretty,
Make it true.

Diagnosis

In my soul a platform or a floor -
Above it total insincerity -
I don't like the people that I like -
Beneath it sewage, sludge and what I feel
And the whole of my intelligence.

The Kiss

(my cat)

Does Maxx know what a kiss is?
Yes, he does.
Did God or evolution teach him this?
The God who'd let him perish
And forget him.
What's the survival value
Of a kiss?

Poetry

A string stretched taut
From bone to bone
Of my skeleton -
I play on it and
Call it poetry.
Does it make a tone
Pleasing anyone? -
A fly in syrup
Struggles to be free.

Five Poems

Look beneath his hoodie
On a winter night and find
The terrifying loneliness
Of a madman's mind.

Beauty is despised.
Insanity is hell.
And poets have so much to say
They needn't say it well.

Looking for a kind of music -
Half-divine and far
Away – another melody
From a distant star.

She's living like a Prince
In the land of milk and honey.
She's sad, so she's entitled
To other people's money.

The kindest person
I've ever seen
Is just as dead
As if she was mean.

For Dory Previn

The rhesus monkey and the cloth mother -
The boy and his teddy bear -
The paper describing Jesus
Tossed into the garbage by mistake
So there is no Jesus anywhere or ever -
Is heaven true
Or do I just want it to be?

Lines

Knocking on the door
Believers wander through -
Just because they say it
Doesn't make it true.

Start with little children;
Get them when they're young.
Tangled up in heaven
After they are hung.

A vista spread before them,
Foggy in a cloud -
They'll never have a thought
That is not allowed.

Hoping for tomorrow
After they are dead -
Science must discover
What Jesus never said.

The Past

More sweet the ones I knew
Than the ones I know!
Distant, distant memory -
Underneath, - a glow -

The mountains that I climbed
And oceans I crossed then
Look impossible to climb
Or cross again.

Lines

So many people inside my head -
I don't know who I am -
I hold back the madness -
The Dutch boy at the dam.

So many thoughts – so many thoughts -
I don't know which are mine -
Crazy thoughts that hate the mobs
That, following a sign,
Kill the gentle,
Rule the world,
And think they are divine -

Truth

In the silent madness of my room,
I sit and pet a calm agnostic cat.
Burning unbelievers, Jews and witches -
Darwin never did a thing like that. -

Truth – Truth – so very many Truths!
None of them's the same for everybody -
Evolution's very interesting -
And religion's very, very bloody.

What?

Pretend that you have money.
It's an easy thing to do
When you're walking down the sidewalk
With a dollar in your shoe.

Billy's very skinny.
Rupert's very fat.
And Tommy with a piece of string
Is playing with the cat.

Standing in the rain
(As foolish as you get!),
He tried to write a poem,
But the paper just got wet.

Housman

Perfect little rhymes
That stud the end of lines -
Phrases of sad music
Like diamonds from mines -

Not every song is sad
(An elegy for death) -
Though every song is beautiful -
And warm, like living breath -

Very gentle beauty
And love in every strain -
Is there genius in a poem? -
Intelligent, humane -

Poe

A moody poet – Poe -
The feeling in his verse
Radiates the glow
Of someone in a hearse.

Little turns of thought,
Phrases too adept,
And melancholy love
With sadness from a crypt -

But less of this than madness,
Sorrowful and sad
And gloomy as a tale
Told by someone mad.

What became of Poe?
Beaten in an alley.
God only gave him tragedy
And love that's melancholy.

The Songwriter

If you dislike my music
It's because you just don't listen.
He said this without laughing.
He was stern.
How hard must I listen to like
Gershwin, Rodgers, Porter,
Loesser, Coleman, Styne,
de Paul or Kern?

Lines on Poetry

A mind that's held together
By dead psychologies
And decaying glue -
Makes the adaptation
To warm mythologies
And low-tided oceans.
Verse forever new!
Imitation life -
And the sea is warm -
Art for only pleasure -
Nothing without form -
To sacrifice my personality
To poetry!

1-3-10

Love

A cat who is crippled or scalded,
Has maybe lost most of his fur,
Still wants to be cuddled and petted,
And when he's happy will purr.

Alone in a wilderness crying,
Caught with compassion and care
By someone who's very much kinder
Than Jesus, who wasn't there.

For Edna Millay

Talent isn't learned.
It's just the way you are.
From the brow of Gods
It springs full grown.
All the brains in Christendom
Do not make a poet.
A light is born in some;
The way is shown.

Lines

Several years on the planet to wonder -
To listen to music,
To look at a statue -
They think they're precocious and gloat,
"I wrote poems in my youth."
Sarah Chang who has talent
Played the violin at 7.
Illusion – not Christ -
Is the Savior.
Conceit keeps artists young.

Lines

How can it be love
If it isn't kind?
Subservience and terror
Eradicate the mind.

In spite of any Gods,
Angels or a Son,
Extremity and horror
Can occur to anyone.

Success

When you write a book
And someone reads it -
Even if he likes it, it's
A temporary love.

Is lonely satisfaction
The extent of your endeavor?
You've written it. It's over.
You're not him. – He isn't you.

After it is done
And those who read it have gone home
To bed – You sit and ask, "Is there
No more to this – than this?"

And despite success –
To please a single person -
He told you it is good; you think,
"But it isn't Keats!"

Heaven

Scarlatti, Clementi, Beethoven, Bach,
Mozart's piano sonatas,
Haydn's piano sonatas -
Let this be my heaven; while preachers
Continue to talk.

Maxx

Maxx, don't be a person;
Stay a cat.
Cover up your poop and sleep
Beside me, purring softly.
The gentle and the beautiful
Are no longer wanted.
At the altar of the ugly
Lies all goodness sacrificed,
Proving even beauty
And its makers
Can be murdered.

Her

"Only God can judge me."
That is what she said -
And took what wasn't hers
Without regret.
Probably her Jesus
Will animate the dead -
A Jesus and a God I never met.
Millenniums! Millenniums! And a thousand Gods!
Trust one –
Or trust another one instead.

Poetry

A poetry of thought -
Not images or music -
Can the thinking of a madman
Who's a fool be interesting?
If it has a little rhythm?
And is this poetry?

Cats

The cat purrs softly like the sea
Sleeping by my head
Underneath the covers.
We are warm instead

Of chilly in the winter
Where the trees are bare
And the grass is frozen.
Another cat is there

Looking through the window,
Hungry, shy and cold.
He took a little food.
He wasn't very old.

Then he went away.
He ate the food and then
Ran back into the darkness.
He'll be here again.

J.S.

I thought there was a person
Very strong and wise -
A mother of the cosmos
In human guise -

Someone who was kind
To catch me when I fall -
With total understanding
Who'd explain it all.

Maybe this is God;
A futile thought because
Millenniums of Gods,
And none that ever was -

The Catatonic

How statuelike I see thee stand,
Sitting in a chair,
Not saying anything,
Not going anywhere;
No expression but a stare.

Laughed the smug psychologist,
"So what if he's insane?
Anyway he's happy."
Though no one could explain,
Then said the catatonic,
"I'm in constant pain."

The Prisoner

A prisoner in a battle
Alone begins to cry
And vomit on himself because
He knows he's going to die.

Looking at the gallows
Through the concrete square
Window of his cell,
With a hollow stare.

Wishing for the God -
In youth a cause of doubt -
He hears the warder's footsteps
Come to lead him out.

Helplessly a man
That only God can save,
Thinks of the unknown,
Beginning with a grave.

Someone

She didn't say "Stop".
She didn't say "No".
She wouldn't;
Or she couldn't.
Believing in phantoms
That disappear
In the air when you're
Not looking.
Tormented and sad -
Too often she smiled.
The church with scorn
Wouldn't take her.
Grateful and pleased
At receiving a gift;
Almost as happy as giving.
Then she died;
She killed herself.
Unhappiness went
To nothing.

MNK

Her caustic jeers and mockery
Echo in my brain.
I went to her for help.
She increased the pain.

Eleven months, a year -
Why did I remain?
That hideous psychologist
Has driven me insane.

I wrote to her employer
And asked him to explain
What she could be doing.
But he didn't answer.

Indifference and cruelty -
And the strong go first -
Purveyors of compassion
Are probably the worst.

The Psychologist

Tell her what you feel
And be extinguished like a flame,
Clobbered by a doctor
Who won't recall your name.

On Being Ripped By A British Vanity Press

Brits are no better than Yankees,
More honest or better read,
Less inclined to be philistines
Or smell any better when dead.

To say that a Brit is more honest
Is a big undeniable fiction.
The English just talk with an accent,
Better grammar and stilted diction.

1971

(at the mental health clinic)

Dennis went for help.
The clinic was unreal.
Everyone deferred
To a performing seal.

Dennis went away.
No one said to wait.
I later read he jumped
From the Golden Gate.

In matters such as this
No one blames the shrink.
The fault must lie with Dennis,
Floating in the drink.

John & Mary

(shrinks)

John and Mary – both of them are gone,
Long ago. Though time continues on,
And like an ocean wave across the shore,
Erases – quoth the Raven, "Nevermore" -

I cannot keep the thought of them at bay -
Or like a wizard, wave them both away.
Like the soft forgetting of the sea,
I'm waiting for the hour I can say,
"The sting is gone. It's just a memory."

"Shine"

I sit alone upon the beach.
Thalassic thunder rolls.
The ocean whispers to the fog,
"Madmen have no souls."

But if they do have hearts and souls
(In ruins and in tatters),
They wander by the sea and ask,
"Whatever really matters?"

Madmen are not brave,
But cowardly and wrong,
Seldom make much sense,
And are not loved for long.

Psychiatry

Psychology. I know
Only what I've read.
They used to knock a hole
In the crazy person's head

To let the demons out.
Or put him on a rack
And hit him with a shock
That often broke his back.

Or stun him with injections.
Or bury him in ice.
The history of psychiatry
Isn't very nice.

Does it clear your mind?
Improve the way you think?
In fact, does it do anything
But make you hate the shrink?

Animals continue.
Only people fall.
If your only hope's psychiatry,
You have no hope at all.

Poetry

The beautiful and true -
This is poetry.
Read the morning papers
If you want reality.

The Statue

Carving at the statue -
Lines upon the face -
Marble legs and torso -
Carefully the hands -
Fingers made of stone -
Rough and grey and smooth -
Working after midnight
Lighted by the moon -
Working in the daylight -
Many many weeks -
Then finished with the statue -
Not another touch
Needed – he had better
Call his work complete.
He stopped and stared exhausted.
It couldn't be improved.
His single great achievement.
He lay beside the statue
And gently went to sleep,
And sleeping, slowly died.
A statue! As if God
Commissioned works of art!
As he rested dead,
The sky above grew darker,
Clouds amassed, black darkness
In the Heathen night.

A rain began to fall
On him beside the statue.
Then a shard of lightning
Shot out and struck the statue
And shattered it to dust.

www.ingramcontent.com/pod-product-compliance
Lightning Source LLC
Chambersburg PA
CBHW022203160726
48282CB00024B/314
* 9 7 8 8 1 8 2 5 3 8 5 9 7 *